The King Returns

Written & illustrated by Rob Sargeant

The King Returns

It's been many years since as a young shepherd boy an angel led me to a manger in Bethlehem where the Messiah was born. I had often wondered what had become of that child, Jesus. Then, one day he came to Jerusalem, riding on a donkey. Crowds of people greeted him, singing, "Hosanna! Hosanna!" They waved palm branches, and threw robes down before him as if he was a king. I was there. We all thought that great change was about to come. But the temple priests weren't ready to receive the rule of Jesus Christ.

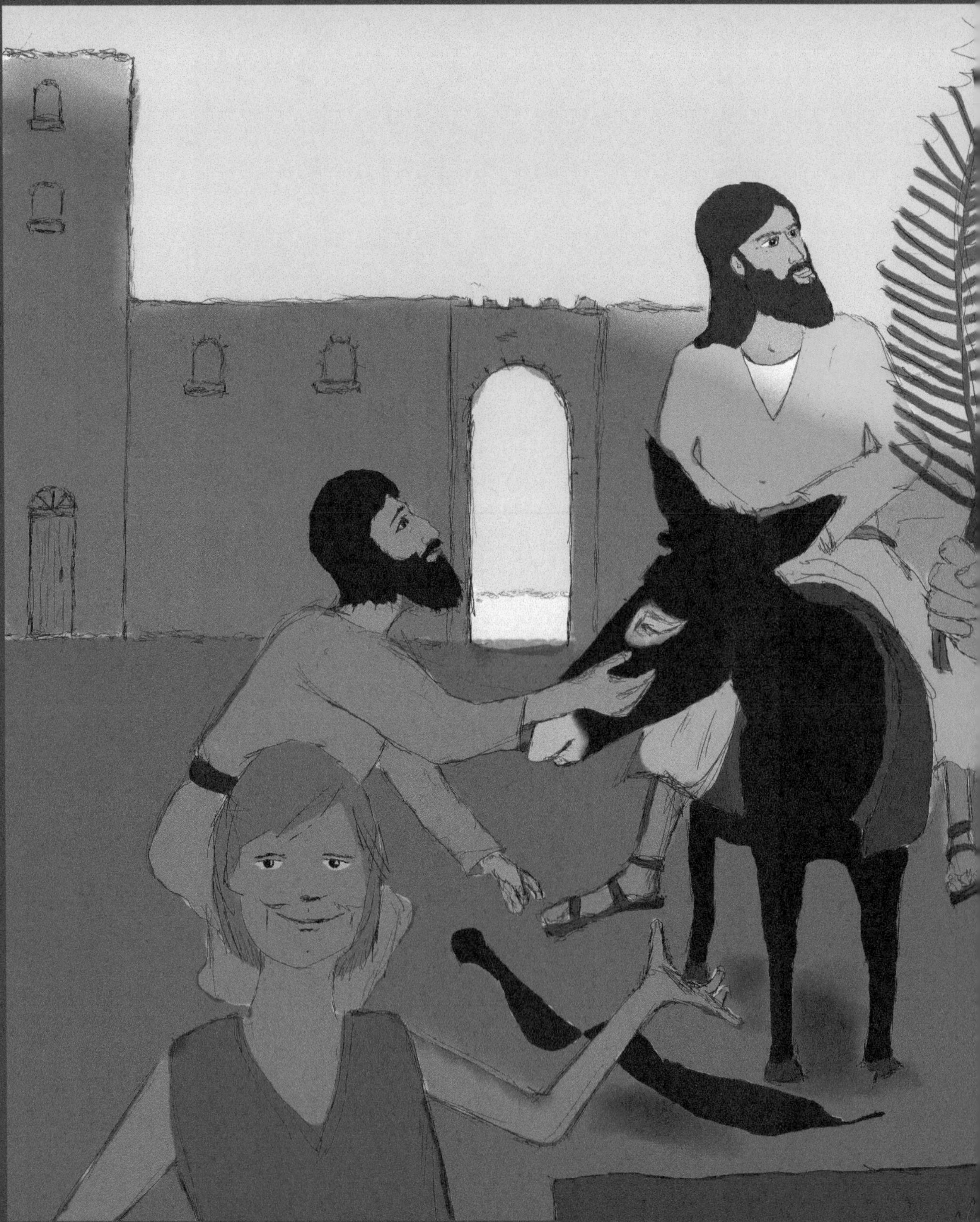

We were surprised to hear that Jesus had been arrested at night. He had a hasty trial before the high priest Caiaphas and Pontius Pilate. By the time I heard news of this, and had traveled from Bethlehem, he was already being led outside Jerusalem's city gates as a man condemned to die. I got there as Jesus struggled to drag a heavy wooden cross up to Golgotha, where the Romans execute the thieves and murderers.

I cried out in protest as he was led through the crowd. Roman soldiers pushed us aside, forcing Jesus to continue. At one point before a steep climb, Jesus fell to his knees, dropping the cross. The soldiers, to help the Lord with his burden, grabbed someone nearby. The man was reluctant at first, but moved by compassion, he took on the weight of the cross. I saw that Jesus was beaten. He wore a crown of thorns.

My cries of his innocence were drowned out by the wailing voices of the women around.

They stopped Jesus near the same spot outside the city where the red heifer was sacrificed - burned by fire until it became ashes. I knew of the tradition, how the ashes of the red heifer were used in the waters of purification. The priests would dip a twig of hyssop into the mixture and sprinkle it upon the unclean to remove their defilement so they could enter the temple. Now I understand the significance of the path Jesus took that day. He became our ongoing sanctifier.

As Jesus lay down on his cross at the top of Golgotha a silence fell across the crowd. We heard his moans as the nails for his hands and feet were pounded in. That's when I realized Jesus was the lamb who would take away the sins of the world. That's why he was born in a manger like thousands of sacrificial lambs before him. Over the course of my life as a shepherd I had witnessed the births and slayings of many. They had to be pure, without blemish, like this man. He had only done good. Voices in the crowd spoke of this.

"Why this? He healed the blind man."
"He raised Lazareth from the dead."
"Cast devils out of the possessed."
"For which of these good things is he being crucified?"

To complete his public display, a Roman soldier nailed a wooden sign into the cross above Jesus' head. It read, "JESUS OF NAZARETH THE KING OF THE JEWS."

Some of his last words were words of forgiveness. He asked his Father to forgive those who had had him crucified. He forgave the thief to his right who repented, and said that day he would later join him in paradise.

Still moved by love and compassion while Jesus was enduring such pain, he asked one of his followers to take care of this mother, Mary, so she would not be alone.

I stayed at Golgotha until the earth shook, and the sky darkened, as Jesus took his last breath. We weren't prepared for the sudden change in the weather. Many of us left after heavy rains began to fall.

I returned to my flock outside Bethlehem.

Three days later I received the good news of Jesus' resurrection. The owner of our flock, a just and devout Jew, came to tell us of how the tomb where the body was laid was now empty. Two of Jesus' female followers, who came to his tomb with spices for his burial, said they met an angel who asked them why they were looking for the living among the dead.

Some of his disciples claimed an angel spoke them. They had seen Jesus risen. They ate with him on different occasions after his resurrection.

I had to see the empty tomb for myself. I went to the garden outside Jerusalem and found it as described. The huge stone was rolled away from its entrance. The residue of a torn Roman seal was still fixed to the rock face above the door. Other people were there too who had heard the news. We all believed Jesus was alive.

"Why look for the living among the dead?"

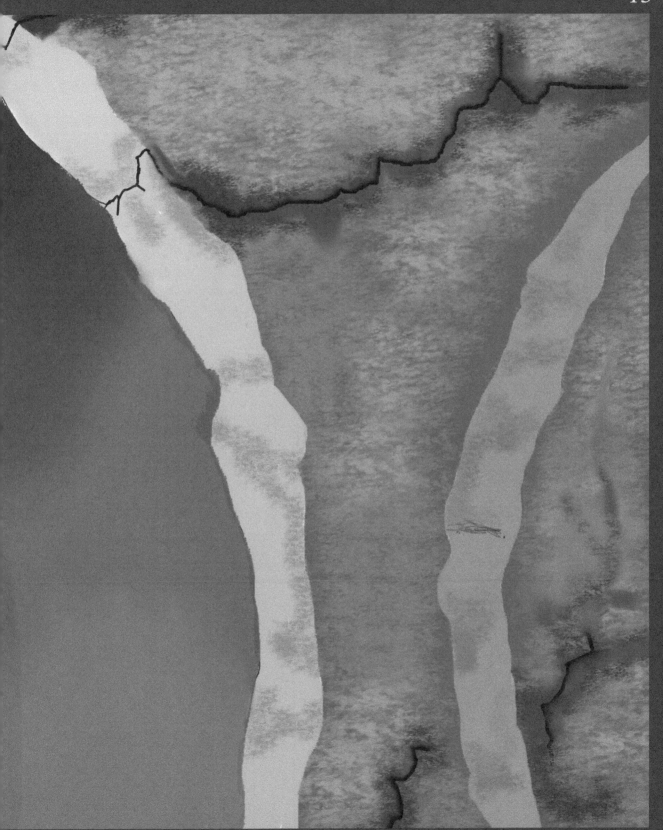

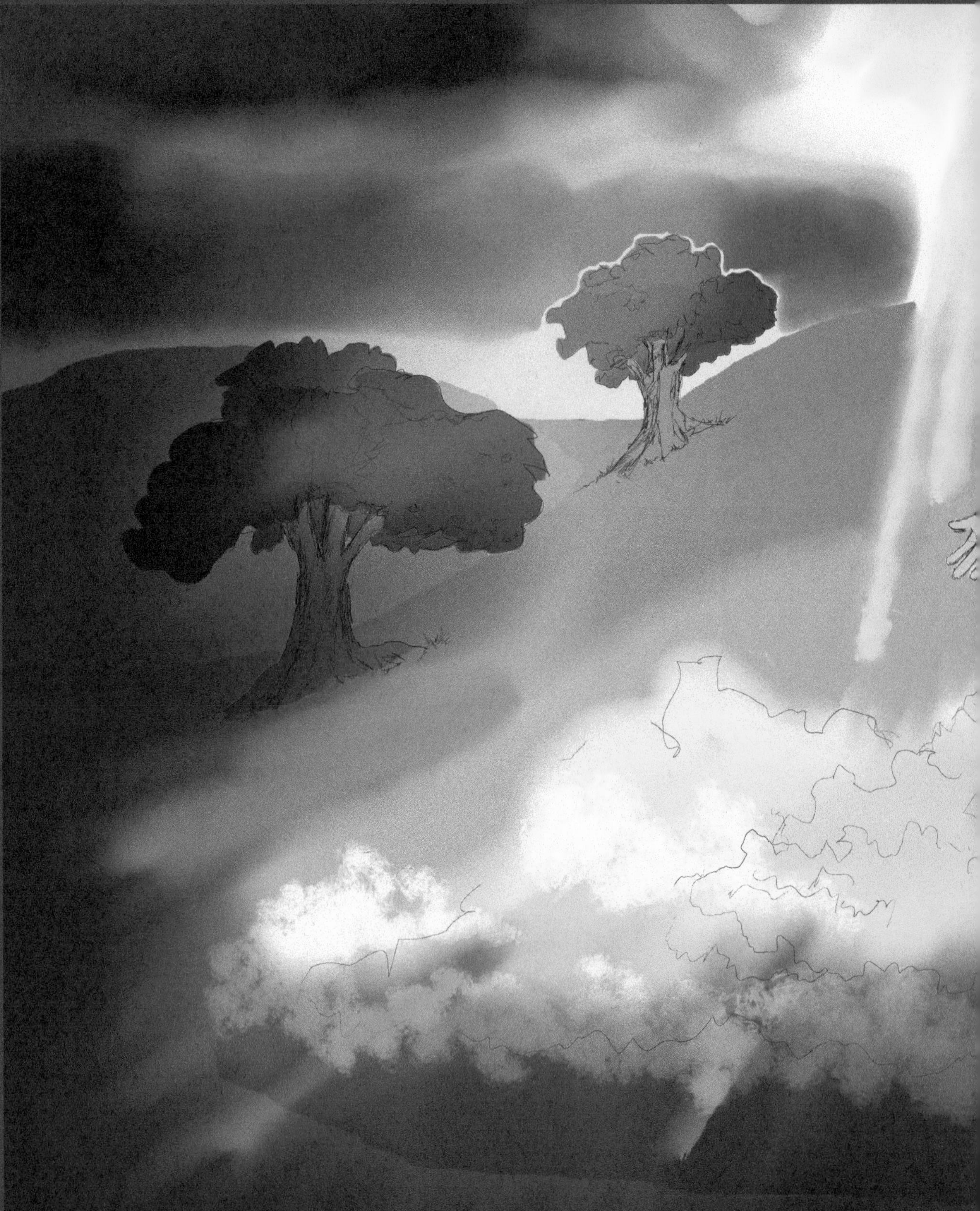

Though I never saw him again I heard that others did in Galilee. His own disciples testified that he appeared to them there as they were fishing. They say he stayed with them for some time.

Soon after this Jesus was caught up into the clouds. As his disciples gazed up to the sky, angels appeared, saying, the same way that Jesus left he would return. I believe this to be true.

Many years have passed since all of these events occurred. I'm still waiting for the return of the king. Maybe it will not happen in my lifetime. The promise could be for a future generation.

The owner of my flock no longer requires me to mark the sheep for tithe. They're not used for sacrifices now because we have faith that Jesus made the final sacrifice for our sins.

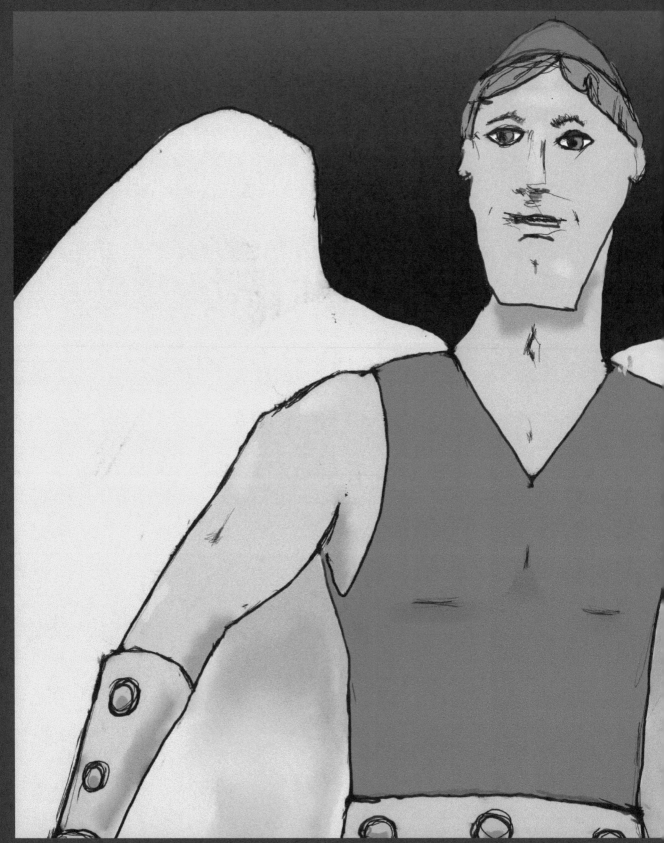

"The same way Jesus left, he will return!"

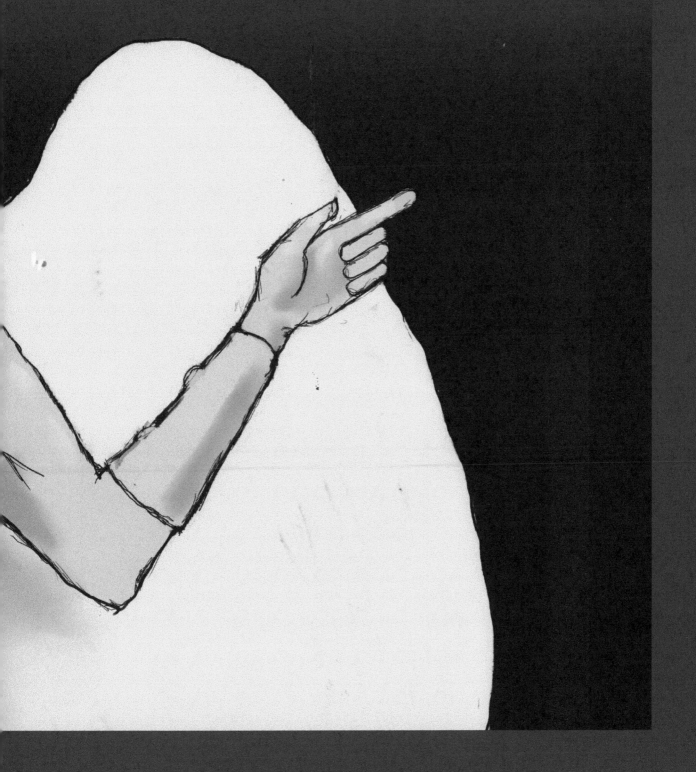

Lightning Source UK Ltd.
Milton Keynes UK
UKHW051144100320
359838UK00010B/73